Angela Gardner

*The Sorry Tale
of the
Mignonette*

Shearsman Books

First published in the United Kingdom in 2021 by
Shearsman Books Ltd
PO Box 4239
Swindon
SN3 9FN

Shearsman Books Ltd Registered Office
30–31 St. James Place, Mangotsfield, Bristol BS16 9JB
(this address not for correspondence)

www.shearsman.com

ISBN 978-1-84861-739-1

Front and back cover from *A Sorry Tale*, folio by Angela Gardner
in the collection of the State Library of New South Wales.

THIS PROJECT HAS BEEN ASSISTED BY THE AUSTRALIAN GOVERNMENT
THROUGH THE AUSTRALIA COUNCIL, ITS ARTS FUNDING AND ADVISORY BODY

Australian Government | Australia Council for the Arts

for my brothers and my sister
Richard, Peter and Jennie

                                        the lights of the lamps
in the windows, call back the day and the dead that
have run away to sea

                        Dylan Thomas
                        Under Milk Wood

'Cannibalism is both a terrible transgression and a strange communion, a human body feeding and sustaining another body.'

                        Rebecca Solnit
                        The Faraway Nearby

CAST

IN ENGLAND & AT SEA

SARAH PARKER cousin of Richard 'Boy' Parker
BOY / RICHARD PARKER Ship's Boy
DANIEL PARKER older brother of Richard
CAPTAIN TOM DUDLEY Captain of the racing yacht *Mignonette*
MATE EDWIN STEPHENS
ABLE SEAMAN NED BROOKS
PHILIPPA DUDLEY wife of Captain Dudley
JIMMY MORRISON and JOHN BURTON, Residents of Falmouth

AT THE TRIALS

SEARGEANT LAVERTY Falmouth Docks
ROBERT CHEESEMAN Collector of Customs Falmouth
SAMUEL JOHN LOUTTIT TRESIDDER Clerk
ERICH WIESE German Sailor from the *Moctezuma*
RICHARD HODGE Licensed Waterman Falmouth
GUSTAVUS LOWRY COLLINS Trinity Pilot Falmouth
MR COLLINS FOR THE DEFENCE Barrister Old Bailey
JUDGE BARON JOHN WALTER HUDDLESTON
THE LORD CHIEF JUSTICE
THE LORD CHIEF JUSTICE'S ASSISTANT
 THE JURY FOREMAN and JURY

IN AUSTRALIA

JACK WANT owner of the yacht *Mignonette*, Barrister and Politician
MARY DUDLEY Captain Dudley's Aunt
TOM DUDLEY'S YOUNG RELATIVE

CONTENTS

Part the First

in which
the characters are introduced

Thin shingle foreshore
between the Mead two buddleia acres
rotting with Bailiff's rent, ragwort
in pence, adding up to mere tidal shillings.
Boats hauled up onto the sloped hard
bass and grey mullet in the estuary
oyster dredgermen in their punts
: the dead-end marsh, late our various industry.
Bounded boats to old Wharfs and drained
a broken pump makes-do, waters feeding
Smith's Mill from the Engine of the Solent.
Storms, tides and shipwrights. Quay and Yard
fishermen, heirs to stumps, nets and oars.

The marsh that lies behind liable
to be flooded and imperfectly drained.

*Richard Parker has been in the shipyards since his parents died. Sarah,
his cousin, lives in the middle of Back Lane, Itchen Ferry, where her
father is a general dealer. It is a poor huddle of dwellings on the edge of
the river mainly occupied by fishermen and their families. The Parkers
are both seventeen with dark-hair and olive skin in a sea of Anglo-Saxon
blondeness.*

*From where she stands Sarah can look across to the docks and shipyards of
Southampton where Richard works at Fay's Yard, a smaller shipyard that
specialises in building racing yachts. Her brother works as a plate-layer,
building the new iron vessels. Before her on this side of the River Itchen:
mud and industry, the timber pool, the slipways and the shipwright's
yards, a new railway. The year is 1884.*

RICHARD
I never saw the treasures you saw at school Sarah
I could never sit still but needed to be doing.

> I want to sail the open promise of the world
> to unfenced miles of silver wheat in waves
> to a strange sun that streams its pan of gold
> to a land that's filled with misfit creatures
> and the coloured parrot birds

> > > > SARAH
> > > > All that's here is tidal salt
> > > > its furbelows and bladderwracks in gaps
> > > > of buddleia, dandelions and ragwort.

RICHARD
And what do I have? From Fay's Yard
past Millstone Point, between the Moulding Loft
and the Galvanising Works.

> > > > SARAH
> > > > Shards and discards, the make-dos and
> > > > the re-makes. On a dead-end broken road
> > > > strewn with the rotting and rusting.

RICHARD
Every day I walk past the open warehouse
and drying floors of Elliot Bros Lime, Brick, Tile & Slate
at Millbank Wharf Hooper and Co. Cement Works
and the petroleum tanks of Jasper Barringer & Sons.

SARAH
All I know of the world is contained
in a box the school mistress showed us.

RICHARD
Scattered oak, elm and beech, the stacks
of Baltic pine and Indian teak, the disused yard
with covered slip and empty launch-way.

SARAH
Gold-leaf & silkworm skeins, broken
cocoons coarse unstoppered. Grained.
Stained Flasks and clear bolls
reels and threads that pile glass, coin the wads
rope felt washed dark of wire, parchment
and motes, wax and silver bubble.

RICHARD
I want riffraff in horn hats and weskits.
Handsome skeletons in jade shoes
and Chinese fingerguards, painted elephants
and telescopes.

SARAH
More likely worsted dull and stiff
than polished plush.
Lustrous, the crystal world's flood fine ebb
ore sawn silver and twisted wool.

RICHARD
Truly Sarah I need more
than the Cement Works' metal crane

and the scrape from the sawpit and the slipway;
the Gasometers and the Coal Yards
the stacks of cement lathes on timber stages
the steam streaming from the joinery.

There's a shimmering land
and sails bound blue
and radiant. Do not tell

but I am to be ship's 'BOY'!

LETTER TO CAPTAIN TOM DUDLEY
FROM HIS AUNT IN SYDNEY 14th March 1884

Such good news that you may come, I felt I must write immediately! We think it a grand plan. We long to see you and your family and being well established here in Redfern can help you settle. I send you some news from Australia: Edward Hanlan, the Canadian oarsman, has arrived here, while Miss Geneviève Ward, the English actress, has made her first appearance in Melbourne, apparently with remarkable success. The Government has commenced an inquiry into Sanitation in Sydney schools. Does Mrs Dudley intend to get work as a teacher when she arrives?

Captain Tom Dudley, red-headed and sturdy, a married man, an Essex man, is in his early thirties. He is God-fearing and tee-total, confident and sober. There has been not enough time for him to have received his aunt's letter. As is often the case their letters will cross in the post.

LETTER FROM CAPTAIN TOM DUDLEY
TO HIS AUNT IN SYDNEY 16th March 1884

Mr Jack Want from Sydney wishes me to sail his new purchased yacht *Mignonette* from Brightlingsea in Essex to Sydney. He is from there but has been sailing the season in England. The money he offers is generous and in truth I am tempted, but the vessel is old and I must engage the crew at my own expense. 52 foot in length and 12 in the beam, she was built by Aldous and her sails are Lapthorne, so that is good. Philippa is teaching in the local school and the children do well. In news from further afield I imagine you read that Major-General Gordon made an unsuccessful sortie from Khartoum, his force being routed and 200 killed while the remainder fled in disorder. It is a bad business.

Here is John Henry Want of Sydney, the registered managing owner.

JACK WANT

> Harbour-side as a pirate bold
> with pickled head I'll seize their hats
> then battle brave in this Golden Age
> I'll plunder and I'll pillage.
>
> Good roguery, single-handedly
>
> a Barrister-turned-Buccaneer
> I have the greatest Want, with
> polished pistol and my cutlass clean
> I'll make 'em walk the plank!

MY *MIGNONETTE*

Port line gleaming
Her, upon delight, soft waves.
Her. Shelter of line gleaming. Her.
Mignonette. Lifting foam to the ! water !
and her pull on, thrusting
upon bright-work. I, she, resistance
: such spring of (old rails)
her line aswish delight. Stripped
feel her resistance.
Her a Her. Yawl I foam against
my giddy breath and soft she
launches great gleaming breaths.
She that swash sea foam her flanks offer
water wake water, wake up!
Streamlined every towards her silk
scantling water to a delight

prow you, resistance line towards yachts
tell the Oh! beauty Oh!
God dances water deck of breath
Oh and at a lifting the wake of when
Oh stiff Even her soft!
Waves towards sea water.
Shelter when Her silk! Wind of rails of hull
She's the prow line wind.
Silk resistance. Pull shipshape, my breath giddy
She takes! God! I clad starboard.
Mizzen, that is how wind awkwards her.
She sails the sea. But the gleaming
Take of and Oh! Like a gleaming.
She's thrusting, when
against even silk starboard resistance
offers delight. Shipshape the rigged mast.
Oh ! prow. *Mignonette,* that God Willing, may bear
the spring of human life.

THE SUMMER RACING SEASON
ON SYDNEY HARBOUR

no guns be fired
no hailing between yachts
no bells rung
no fireworks displayed

At a signal in a single open line
the yachts sail both picturesque and beautiful.
We round a buoy to fly before the freshening wind
down harbour to the turning point. Through
Sow and Pigs reef, around Pinchgut
and the bombora or sunken reef off Dobroyd Point.

The sailors smart in a plain dress coat and fine waistcoat.
By Royal warrant trousers blue or white according to season
on the water with whatever sails the owners please.

Such a wealth of sailing to the day's finishing line:
there are dock owners
and doctors, directors of banks, of coal mines. Colonial
sugar refiners, successful city merchants, the secretaries
of Marine Assurance companies and barristers.
And for the winners a handsome purse.

On Anniversary Day and Hunters Hill Regattas members
are piped down to lunch and to fortify themselves below.
At Hunters Bay below the Nurses Cottage the boat crews
bathe naked. Seen through field glasses the ladies arrive
under steam and refreshments served with dancing.

SAILING THE HARBOUR

It's not all racing, there are
parties and picnics, dramas and dress-ups.
Over there the ladies seated with cups of tea
and the men lounging with bottles of wine.
At our ease in soft linen trousers and neckerchiefs
in straw boaters, moustachioed or bearded
as beer cools beneath crisp white tablecloths.
We explore, pleasure sailing, the harbour's inlets
and private coves, its wooded slopes and beaches.
Impromptu fishing lines dangle over the side.
Here is a photograph of the crew under the sails
and here on the shore mock jousting with oars.
Clark and Shark islands are excellent spots
as are Forty Baskets and Sirius Cove,
but we have our own names:
                                Cara-Bella for Kirribilli
it sounds so well. Oh! we are such wags.

JACK WANT

Oh! I'll give you the bare bones
and the breeze that blows
for I'm restless for adventure.

LETTER TO CAPTAIN TOM DUDLEY
FROM HIS AUNT IN SYDNEY 10th April 1884

Major-General Gordon should be in the Soudan soon. I am sure they are looking forward to seeing him as we are to seeing you. Did you accept the commission from Mr Want? He is well known in Sydney, being a barrister and a member of the Legislative Assembly of New South Wales.

Oh! and I know you will like this piece of news! A sensational race occurred in Port Phillip between the steamers *Wairarapa* and *Adelaide*, ending in a slight collision!

LETTER FROM CAPTAIN TOM DUDLEY
TO HIS AUNT IN SYDNEY 30th April 1884

I have accepted Mr Want's offer, he appears showy but the voyage suits my purpose of starting a new life with my family in Sydney. Now that I know I am coming I find I seek out news of the colonies. For example, I read the Eight Hours Anniversary was celebrated with unusual éclat and last year the yield of wheat in the Australian colonies to be 13 million bushels. I can hardly conceive how large the wheat fields must be!

LETTER TO CAPTAIN TOM DUDLEY
FROM HIS AUNT IN SYDNEY 15th April 1884

Hanlan gave an aquatic exhibition before about 10,000 spectators at Manly on Sydney Harbour and I was there! We were in raptures, the Harbour looked so beautiful. But in sobering news the *R.M.S. Rome* arrived at Queenscliff (near Melbourne) with smallpox on board, let us hope it does not spread to Sydney.

LETTER FROM CAPTAIN TOM DUDLEY
TO HIS AUNT IN SYDNEY 10th May 1884

Give me a sailing ship over a steam ship any day! Speaking of infernal machines there have been discoveries of such (and dynamite!) made in London at the railway stations and an attempt on the life of the Prince of Wales. We sailed from Brightlingsea but have put in to Southampton for some repairs and to engage new crew so we are almost on our way! I write while I am waiting for this to take place and I expect to be here no more than ten days.

CAPTAIN

There's Fay's
and the Arrow Yard. Cutters and refits
yachts like the *Mignonette*, the *Walrus* a yawl
for a Gentleman in Bitterne and a steam launch
Blunderbuss

.

Mignonette at Fay's Yard is high on solid jigs
the new gunwale is clamped
while carpenters crawl under her backbone
to replace any weakness in her ribs.
She's a cruiser, Brightlingsea built
of nineteen tons burden. Yawl rigged
and only to Southampton and in need of repairs.
The Frost brothers who sailed with me
have left the ship and would not sail her further.
I must engage a new mate a Mr Edwin Stephens.
And now Brooks, a new sign-on, is refusing to board.
Maybe he's been talking to the Frost brothers?
For he says she *does not command general confidence*
with a view to the preservation of human life.
I persuaded him not to walk for he had signed
and the Harbour Police would pursue him.
Then there's Richard Parker the Cabin Boy
he's big and able, eager and adventurous.
And it's a great little sea boat but rather old
that God Willing may bear the spring of the frames.
The solid weight in the middle of extra stores and tanks
: her hull trimmed with lead so she may float level
while her mizzen mast is removed leaving her awkward
and now cutter rigged.

The rowing boat is inshore,
scantling clad, flinch flimsy and stiff.

Jack wants what Jack wants
and what Jack wants is a yacht
on the Harbour

on Sydney Harbour.

SCALE OF DAILY PROVISIONS

Sunday Bread 1 lb, Beef 1½ lb, Flour ½ lb
Monday Bread 1 lb, Pork 1 ¼, Peas ⅓ pint, Tea ⅛oz, Sugar 2oz,
        Water 3 quarts
Tuesday Bread 1 lb, Beef 1½ lb, Flour ½ lb,
Wednesday Bread 1 lb, Pork 1¼
Thursday Bread 1 lb, Beef 1½ lb, Flour ½ lb
Friday Bread 1 lb, Pork 1 ¼, Peas ⅓ pint
Saturday Bread 1 lb, Beef 1½ lb, Peas ⅓ pint

Substitutes at Master's Option

The *Mignonette* sailed from Southampton on 19th May 1884 with a crew of four:

Captain Tom Dudley
Mate Edwin Stephens
Able Seaman Ned Brooks
Cabin Boy Richard Parker

This at last is Richard's escape to other-wheres, his mind floating, no longer held back by the low dank riverbank. He has signed up as an Ordinary Seaman, yet they call him Boy.

BOY

Itchen Ferry is my home.
> *Heave away, Heave away.*

Itchen Ferry is my home.
> *And we're bound for Sydney Harbour.*

> *Heave away, Heave away*
> *Oh! heave away on the Solent tide*
> *for we're bound for Sydney Harbour.*

I see my girl upon the quay.
> *Heave away, Heave away.*

My girl's in tears upon the quay.
> *But we're bound for Sydney Harbour*

> *Heave away, Heave away*
> *Oh! heave away on the Solent tide*
> *for we're bound for Sydney Harbour.*

DANIEL

    Signed on without permission
    and being illiterate could not sign his name.
    He is an orphan.

SARAH

    Poor boy.
    He is determined to make his mark.

BOY

    For I am old enough and strong enough
    to do a man's work.

> *Farewell and adieu to our fair River Itchen*
> *Farewell and adieu to old Southampton Town*
> *For we've set our sails to cross the wide Ocean*
> *And to make for Australia our course it is bound*

SARAH

    And pray God bring Richard home on guiding chains.

Part the Second

in which
the yacht *Mignonette* sets sail for Sydney

BOY

    All hands on deck
    salute the adventurous day.

    How the sails do flap
    and fill with wind.

    Washing day sheets
    to answer the wave

    given by her pale
    handkerchief.

SARAH

    So keen to be away
    so carefree and jaunty

BOY

    Not so sad Sarah
    I trust in the master

    and all shall be right
    for 'tis a grand adventure.

The sea this morning lies silent,
flickering in the light.

Shoreline,
then high ground, or clouds

that could be the sight of land.

Edwin Stephens, the replacement Mate casts a taciturn and world-weary
eye over the departure.

MATE
> Across the bay's cloudy backdrop
> that which is solid, rendered invisible
> it is as if the land only sometimes exists.

NED
> 39 years of age and a Seaman for nigh on thirty.
> I am Able as in Able Seaman on the Yacht *Mignonette*.

He is a sailor unable to swim

> These last 12 years I've known Tom Dudley by reputation
> as a good skipper, and so I've found him.
> But the Frost brothers jumped ship and so should've I.

The captain is persuasive and the Water Police stand by.

MATE
> Only the seabirds to pipe us aboard.

CAPTAIN
>   Dry for the most,
> dull, but fine and pleasant, a gentle northerly veering
> east south east. The head rope that's rove on a slip
> about to be cast-off.

BOY

> On deck, we weigh anchor, leave
> the marshy flood, foreshore of the Itchen.

Light strikes objects in the seabed
its shoals and channels. Southampton docks
at deepwater is a scurry of porters unloading.

> The low brown cliffs
> and narrow sand beaches behind us.

Out past the way markers
and the horizon opening.

CAPTAIN

> The pilot boat beside us so close we can call across.

Seagulls fly low, wheel across their prow.
Fishing boats and ferries, flash along beside.
Isle of Wight steam packets ply
while the boats in the Hamble, shelter.

BOY

> Pleasure yachts in the channel out from Buckler's Hard

Sails reefed as the inshore vessels turn
to Portsmouth and the Naval Yards.

MATE

> The old Queen unseen at Osborne House in seclusion
> and in like-wise the Coast Guard, watching from their
> shore station.

Clippers and new steam-powered ships
bound for Southampton. Breakwater rocks
and bathing sheds along New Forest beaches.
Then they turn at the point where terns skim
water smooth and green, lifting into wavelets.

BOY

    Until we leave the Solent and sail for open water

where the little bays and inlets are too distant
and only the cliffs are visible.

SARAH

Where do you sail as harbour lights fade?
Over soft silts on the long double tide.

Where do you sail as harbour lights fade?
Along a water's edge of weed and wrack.

BOY

On past Pier Head
Where the gulls swim and the grey mullet fly.

Onto the Yarmouth Roads
Where the wind steals their farewells.

Beyond the Hook
As the breeze shifts offshore amid restless swells.

SARAH

Where do you sail now that harbour lights fade
and the halfmoon flies from the bowsprit?

BOY

On sea-charts we plot a southern route
just a compass span on the chart to Madeira.

SARAH

Oh! a cold wind carries all before it
as at last light you reach the restless water.

BOY

But *the Needles light burns in the night*
as we farewell the shifting Shingles Bank
and the whole ocean of the world is ahead
out to the grey Atlantic.

CAPTAIN

At sea May 21st at 10.30 am boarded the Schooner Yacht *Lady Eleven* and put letters into their hands and got a little water from them.

LETTER FROM CAPTAIN TOM DUDLEY
TO HIS AUNT IN SYDNEY 21st May 1884

Dear Aunt I write in haste to say 'All's Well.' We are underway and have had good sailing weather. We have met at sea the Schooner Yacht *Lady Eleven* whose captain has said he will take letters to post to tell of our good progress.

BOY

> The voyage out
> we sailed as fine
> and fair as fivepence.

SARAH

> I think of you Richard. How
> day and night; in heat and cold
> all the energies of tossing and collapse
> in the waters of a gentle swell. How
> in the Atlantic's long intervals
> and in tropic brilliance the *Mignonette*
> floats charmed on clear water
> that's skittish in the breeze.

BOY PARKER AT EIGHT BELLS

And at watch Eight Bells
lashed dark and a weather sea from the slop edge.
On deck everything reflects the swaying moon
the lamps Sea-light, night all buoys trim incantation
and the bells roar clouded. Salt bustles the breeze
the captain polishes intervals to starboard
rigging dream-soaked on sharp heat. Wind tosses
the smooth collapse. Bow-wave, wind skittish
darker brilliance and at tarry hammocks prow.
The gentle dark under doldrum drifts and tropic night.
We wake charmed to sea-glass, clear knife of waves
energies and water. Our tang of bright briny
as she floats on sunlight.

SIGNALLING

Where are you bound?
We are bound to Sydney
On the weather bow

When the breeze springs up
The breeze will freshen
The breeze will die away

After dark
At daylight
The decision is final

What has happened?
Up the harbour
Down the harbour

Keep near to me
I will hoist a light during the night

BOY

A score of whales plunge beside us
with a tremendous snorting and blowing.
One monster crosses so close to our bows
there seems no escape from hitting him.
Another took a dive right under
and, coming up the other side, spouted
giving us a drenching.

CAPTAIN
At sea Sunday 14ᵗʰ June we hailed and boarded the British ship *Pride of Lorne* 42 days from Cardiff, Captain Fraser kindly took letters for us.

LETTER FROM CAPTAIN TOM DUDLEY
TO HIS WIFE PHILIPPA IN SUTTON
Sunday 14ᵗʰ June

Dear Wife I write to say 'All's Well.' We live a different life on board but it is comfortable. We make great headway, the weather is kind to us, and we are under sail in the *Mignonette* with high hopes of seeing our Australian family within months in Sydney. As soon as I am there and settled, I will pay for a passage for you and our dear children to come as well.

CAPTAIN
At dawn I took our position by the sight of five stars
        by sextant and chronometer.
At noon I took our latitude from the sun.

BOY

>I looked at the stars in the sky
>and a great emptiness above
>stared back an ocean to me.
>
>I looked at the lights in the ocean
>and a great emptiness beneath
>reflected a night full of stars.

NED

> We called at Madeira.

BOY

> Before the daylight fled
> we saw birds and a distant group of islands.
> Four dark brooding hulks rose
> cliffed and mysterious and green
> the scent of flowering trees and earth.
> Last lights on land faintly glowed.
> How am I to sleep?

CAPTAIN

> 1st July at midnight took in water
> and a little fresh meat.

BOY

> At dawn on deck to look
> but after I had the breakfast made
> allowed to wander for an hour.
>
> The white painted squares
> where dark eyed flower girls
> call to me to ply their wares.

CAPTAIN

> I took the opportunity to cable
> to my wife Philippa 'All is well'
> We left again 2nd July at noon.

In July the weather worsened.

CAPTAIN

> We run before a growling wind
> making no headway
> in seas that are bumpy and rising
> and our eyes are pelted with rain.

MATE

> All day and all night it howls
> and the sea towers above us
> harder and harder blows the wind.

NED

> The night very dark, the water
> murky and the wind variable
> : gusts of it tearing at the sails.

CAPTAIN

> Unsettled
> we take in all sail
> with intent to ride out the gale.
> We double reef our mainsail
> in heavy squalls the weight of clouds
> thrashing her body and ours.

> A great wind and her to spindrift
> crowning the sails with spume and lash.
> The rain swell night very growling.
> Unsettled squalls full scud
> that tear at eyes in gusts.
> We smash through trough and crest.

RUNNING BEFORE THE STORM

Clouds gather thick upon us
and the wind it sings astern
the storm is a restless tumult
a darkness formed in hell.

A dreadful roaring comes by fits
it beats the light from heaven.
There's nothing for to comfort us
and nothing left of hope.

Troubled and overmastered
it loathsomely effects its powers
: a sickness insufferable of the body
as our senses storm the mind.

The world turns black upon us
by horror and fear overrun
our ears are laid open with cries
that works upon each one.

The sea runs too high
before the wind.

CAPTAIN
> It blows!

MATE
> It blows too hard.

> Can you see?
> How is she standing?

> > *Squally weather*
> > *Before the storm.*

> We are so far away and yet
> so far to go

> > *Into the barb of the wind*
> > *howling, roaring and beating.*

> > *The little yacht strains*
> > *Plumbs each treacherous wave.*

> > *She rolls violently*
> > *on the dead weight in her belly*

> > *the new lead in her keel.*

5th July 1884 at 27°10′ south and 9° 50′ west

CAPTAIN

    Look out Mate! Here it comes
    — take the jib off
    — douse your mizzen
    — double-reef your mainsail

suddenly she was shipping it green
wave-struck
the waters of the deep, with no let
or hindrance, flow over her completely.

CAPTAIN

    I catch hold of the boom to steady me
    with it coming down on top of us

Down and into it we went
a wave as high as a church steeple
chucks her bows up

    and lets her down
            with a bang.

Out of the chasm she comes
wire guys and hob-stays
banging alongside,
the wreckage of ironwork
half the bowsprit
and the spar
broken under the weight of water.

I wonder it did not break the boom
as its fearful weight carries away
her stanchions and lee bulwarks, turning her sideways.
Above the fearful wind it shatters and loosens
we hear the stern frame roar
as it gives way.

BOY

> The deafening rush. She lists
> I am breathless, my heart hammering.
> Her rail is almost flat to the brine
> as a wall of water smashes into me
> and knocks my feet from under me.

CAPTAIN

> She is filling with water.
> Her back is broken.
> No time for lifebelts
> no time to signal.

BOY

> Everything goes: the pots
> and pans, the plates and bowls, the knives
> and spoons. Her hull ruptures
> and her rudder breaks. My insides loosen
> as planks float across the water and I am
> in a vivid fearful expectation.

NED

> Move lad move, get into the boat.

CAPTAIN

> No time to be stupefied or terror-struck
> I enter the Cabin up to, then above, my waist
> throw some tins, the breaker of sweet water, the binnacle
> and the sextant to navigate, into the boiling sea.

MATE

God have mercy,
the rowing boat is ready but holes as she hits the water.

NED

> Me, the mate, and the boy are in the boat
> I call to the captain to come.

Come! Come! I call. I despair he will ever come.
Save us Oh Lord, or else we perish.

MATE
We are pitching heavily, the mountainous ocean
breaching over us.

BOY
        and then the world dissolves
until I can no longer see.

THE DROWNED YACHT

Into this thrashing, upon the leaden mind,
the brine black storm astern it

our high seas, our heavy seas
darkness into ropes and her pale canvas filling

streaming bubbles of bright air along her bow
into the whirlpool

Unloosed, her huge strung sails gone
the masts engulfed, she sails into the long emptiness

sails carrying air, carrying everything drowning

… down
      into
         dark
            receding

               away

                  into the depths

BOY

Five pence to spend
and five pence to lend

Adrift on an inked skin of ocean
a hand on a rope, an anchor
a sailing ship or mermaid.
MOTHER!
Oh! we are marked
indelibly. How she gets under my skin
the cold South Atlantic.

Nothing salvaged, the fresh water lost
and but two small tins of turnips.

SEND ME A BOAT

Have you sustained damage?
I have sustained damage

It is very dangerous
My boat is swamped

Are you in distress?
Boat cannot pull against sea or wind

It is by no means certain
Send me a boat

Have you any fresh water?
There is no water

Have you any oars?
Please God I cannot

If I cannot
Can you?

Part the Third

in which
we contemplate the aftermath of the shipwreck
and a most ghastly murder

LETTER TO CAPTAIN TOM DUDLEY
FROM HIS AUNT MARY IN SYDNEY
12th June 1884

I fear that my letter will cross with yours due to the length of time it takes your letters to come from home but I send this last letter. Our family does well and we look forward to seeing you. A ship's chandlery business is available. I will give you particulars when you arrive. There has been a plague of mice in the Wimmera district. I find I cannot abide the thought of them. It is as I feared: there has been much agitation caused in Melbourne by cases of an eruptive disease resembling small-pox, I just only hope it does not reach Sydney.

CAPTAIN

    Our position very bad. Night
    and four of us in a small boat
    the seas come on mountains high.
    A great sea that fills her up.
    It is dreadful,
    water comes in faster than we can bail.
    It seems our time is near.

MATE

    We look to the Captain, who scours
    the surface for broken timbers.

    Each now reaches for anything floating
    to lash with a shroud line as a sea-anchor
    and hold our little rowing boat to the wind.

BOY

    Rain falls, as through the very windows
    of heaven. The boat is pushed back by wind
    and wave but the bow now holding steady.

NED

    That first night the seas roil beneath us

MATE

    and fills the boat to the gunwales,
    we are soaking wet as we bail and bail.

BOY

    Jarring fright and deep distress
    the hollow moans of wood and wind
    muffling my cries.

MATE

    An unrelenting struggle in and on the raging
    we roll and sink, the small boat valleys
    with nothing for the anchor to bite.
    A fell storm ploughs the phosphorescence
    we roaring and a tremble, the brim unrelenting
    water in the boat up to the gunwales
    so we are soaking wet, exhausted
    and we must bail and bail.

That night came a great shark nearly as long as their boat smacking and knocking his tail under them.

CAPTAIN
A Monster like him near us
desiring of our bodies
I pray we might be spared to see
all at home and live a better life.

MONSTER OF THE DEEP

Just a flick of his tail
that shook the boat from stem to stern
we feared his powerful jaws
how a shark could
       rip our limbs from our body
       strip the flesh from our bones
       tear out our abdomen and viscera
       leave us bloody or drowned.

He shook me
voracious him, monster lunging and blind
Open-mouthed to strip us with jaws.
His body broke the ocean from the stern.

       His eye, his huge eye,
       passes just beside me.

Eye him, hit, struck eye. We attack
the shark, a rip of fear seizes bold limbs.
We hit the brute all drowned Blind-sided
We are afeared of his return. That it ends so.
Beside bones huge beam powerful, threw him
and his bailer, fear below that nearly cast again
tear with rush, passes the mortal of us.

We hit him with the bailer and an oar.
We hit him again and again in fear of our lives
We hit him and hit him
until the monster leaves us to the ocean.

MATE
    If we could have killed
    …and eaten him

The boat drifts upon the endless ocean
more than a thousand miles from land.

CAPTAIN
>   Below the awful blackness of the sky

>   and beneath me a dark chasm of water opens
>   then a shower of gold, a farthing scramble.

>   And I, overcoming a void more terrifying, saw
>   the continuous expanse in which all things exist.

>   Yet I saw nothing but water. Boundless,
>   deeper and deeper beneath me, the waves

>   on the ocean lit for miles with a phosphorescence
>   that flames over the face of the abyss.

AN INCOMPLETE SUMMONS

Came the cry 'man overboard!'
The small boat's quick-jumps pitched him
headlong into the raging waters.
An interruption of water and air
our two worlds turned inside out
and shown double-sided. Ned is fallen
into the sea and all is in such confusion
beneath us.

His panic trembles the water
he sinks unable to swim
but kicks and struggles
brim and brink
against his own absolute need
to live.

A glance to leeward and he reappears
into air in a rupturing swell and surge
: the surface all froth and thrash.
And as she rolls to leeward the wash
throws him back over the edge. Nothing else
could save him, for he could not swim.
And we haul him through the soft
encompassing belly of the water
wet and flapping and onto deck.

NOT YET

Lost overboard
Washed overboard
Fallen overboard

We are not able
If we are able
Are you able?

All saved
Nobody saved
What did he say?

We are unable
It is very uncertain
Do you understand?

The day before yesterday
It is not yet
Not yet.

It took days to find the hole and stop the great rush of water and they all offered up prayers to be brought through their present danger.

CAPTAIN

> And sure I am that they were heard.
>
> We trust to God to take care of us
> and that night He ruled the seas.
> The most remarkable thing
> it was Wonder full.
> For the waves would break
> within a foot of the little boat's bow
> when we thought they would engulf us
> and our time was come.
>
> Save us Oh Lord, or else we perish.

They did not touch the turnips for 3 days.

turnip
for the boredom of days counting down to what?
for two tins of turnips that were all we had
for the shark that hungrily circled us
for not enough to live for a weevil
for the sea-birds out of reach
for our diminishing hope
our hunger and thirst
a blank horizon
or fading light
for nights
and days
on end
less.

On the fourth or fifth day they caught a turtle, which lasted until the eleventh day. They drank its blood & then ate it, but lost the biggest part of the blood through the seawater.

MATE

    Oh! a turtle is the best of fish

BOY

    better than a puffin!

MATE

    Lift her into the boat boys
    though she's made of tough old boots.
    Tear the flesh from out her shell.
    We'll chew her leathery skin, boys.

BOY

    Oh! a turtle is the best of fish
    better than a puffin!

MATE

    Eat the flesh and chew the skin
    Don't let her slip down to the water

    For a turtle is the best of fish
    better than a puffin!

CAPTAIN

    We were so over joyed
    that we ate our second tin of turnips.

    And no-one can think how sweet
    they went down our parched throats
    but ourselves.

NED

in the emptiness
the many fathoms
of the fathomless
I slip my moorings
to the endless ocean
below.

They had no water, save some rain that fell, and they drank their own urine, not the boy, though they do urge him.

SHODDY TARNISHED GIFTS

No-one but us, on an empty horizon.
We are thrown into a terrible wilderness.
Our shredded shirt sail lolls in its open window
of sky (filthy old rags) above paths
of the sea unmade and purposeless.

Another day, the sun a howling mouth
our lips a wasteland. Unable to speak
throats filled with stones, tongues swollen
in our mouths. Lips black and cracked
limbs gross and becoming useless.

The shoddy, tarnished gifts of shiny
mottled skin taut with iron barbs, tight
and seared with pain.

CAPTAIN
We are wretched in a wasteland of howling winds.
Filled with humiliation and vexation.
– didn't I set the right course?

For though we were spared we are roughcast
rowers over endless fathoms, endless fatigue
– didn't I set the boom?

For the water that surrounds us is a sorrow,
we look for rescue but find further peril
– didn't I make a sea anchor?

For what is recovered from the wreckage
will not be replenished from elsewhere
– didn't I do enough to prepare?

For when the shark circles beneath us sensing
Blood and its maw opens to saw-like shears
– didn't I hold it off?

I have made no enemies, I have saved my sailors
And I think on our wives and children
– aren't we clinging: drowning men to wreckage?

In the rowboat in silence. Our mouths are dry.
Our minds drift, drift on the ocean
– isn't this a shipping lane

                              and rescue will come?

SARAH

And will you turn for home Richard?
To rough pasture, to a pear tree, thin
and stony flanks of toadflax to ox
-tongues, mulleins and soapwort.
And yellow in weak sunlight
      the wild mignonette.

So much depends upon the wind
unloosed upon the early hair grass.
Hidden sheep's sorrel below hedged
elms, mustard and mugwort.
A cold wind blows over the reeds
      and codlins.

And are you coming home?
To tides of sun and the waves
of grass that topple in the wind.
Below Hill Road, the sea path
of wayside weeds, their scent
      a ragged bewilderment.

MATE

> Still the endless empty horizon
> and the boy, who will not drink
> > as we have learned to
> > (as we must do)
> the water of our own bodies

BOY

> I'd rather drink the salt of the sea.
> That foul odour! And nowhere
> to get from the shame and the filth.
> They say I must, but how could I?
> I see their disgust, the clenched nostrils
> the pursed lips. How they would puke
> it out, though they would hide it.

MATE

> for in our clinging will
> we must drink humiliation.

BOY

> In fury and fear
> fouled and fisted
> we sailed as false
> and fraudulent
> as fivepence.
>
> Nothing salvaged
> the voyage falters
> the fresh water lost
> and the two small tins
> of turnips all gone.

CAPTAIN

To whoever picks this up / Sunday July 20th PM / We Thomas Dudley, Edwin Stephens / Ned Brooks & Richard Parker, / the crew of the Yacht Mignonette which / foundered on Saturday the 5th. of July, have / been in our little dinghy 15 days. We have / neither food or water and are greatly reduced / We suppose our Latitude to be 25º South our Longitude / 28º West. May the Lord have mercy upon us / please forward this to Southampton.

BOY

      I am afraid.

NED

      I am here.

MATE

    days on the ocean
    nights on the ocean
    nothing changes
    nothing unchanging
    except our raging thirst.

NED

    Adrift we lay down
    in a delirium and dream of rescue.
    Over me, tides and currents of a dream Atlantic
    somewhere between Saint Helena and Tristan
    da Cunha. Sleepless I wake and the wind
    is sung with songs I dare not fathom.

CAPTAIN

    There are terrors
    the anchor sways its dead-weight.

    Wind scoured. A speck of flotsam
    the ocean ignores.

    Useless and derelict
    all certainties gone on this brutal salt.

    Beyond the missing outline of coast
    we are set apart and without rescue.

They found they had driven & sailed a thousand miles from where Mignonette *foundered. Thinking every wave, being mountains high, would swamp them.*

CAPTAIN
> [to suffer as we poor souls did]

POOR MISFORTUNE

As if Saint Helena island was set adrift
and scoured alive we sail a salt. Come my Sleepless boat.
Derelict we dare the ocean, them mermaids being in dreams,
in Atlantic songs. Delirium, cold, its skin a thousand terrors
and we a dead-weight. What poor misfortune!
to hope a ship will come. Oh! … from somewhere we dream
our souls awake and they a speck in seas below
as ocean mountains marked, we trust upon God's chart –
waiting for a morning to break to see a remarkable coast.

On the 18ᵗʰ day, after 7 days without food and 5 without water, the Captain and Mate spoke to Ned.

CAPTAIN
> Stephens. How many children have you?

MATE
> Five & a wife.

CAPTAIN
> I have three and a wife

> > CAPTAIN & MATE
> > What should be done if no succour comes?
> > Someone should be sacrificed to save the rest.

NED
> I should not like to kill anyone
> and I should not like anyone to kill me.

The boy (they refer to) lies at the bottom of the boat, not consulted.

> *Richard is losing the north*
> *as the pole star dips down*
> *to the southern cross.*
>
> *The untethered stars*
> *drifting in constellations*
> *across the sky.*
>
> *By day the sea braids like hair*
> *perplexing paths*
> *far from safe harbour.*
>
> *By night when the monsters rise*

BOY

> They speak about me secretly
> nodding and glancing.
>
> I huddle in the bottom of the boat
> and pretend they cannot see me.
>
> Oh Sarah! I have no more tears
> to cry my body aches with thirst.
>
> Deep, deep, horror and darkness.
> What have I done?
>
> I never knew how deep.

SARAH

> Jack Want's bought himself a yacht
> to sail out to Sydney town
> (oh Richard Parker stay at home, stay at home)

A cabin boy from Southampton port
out in the south Atlantic
(oh Richard Parker stay at home, stay at home).

For where are you now, my cousin
Oh where are you now, my cousin?
adrift in the wild Atlantic.

THE WATERY GYRE

their imaginary lines
shift somehow over floating islands in their watery gyre.

Ahead there is a different night they travel towards
in turbulence, and deep trenches of their imaginings
so lost now they are close to death. Only the music

in their ears prevents them contemplating the pressured hours
ahead. At its hilltops they sleepwalk an open landscape of sky
chase shadows across the clouds

where the bruised petals
of their mouths half open, half stuck together, are not equal
to the silences or the notes that rise under the singing water

beneath them.

Days and Nights on the Ocean.

Nights and Days on the Ocean.

BOY

      the days are so long
      and my thirst is so great.
      I drank of the sea,
      and now I am sick.

Richard lies in the bottom of the boat in a delirium. He no longer knows water from dry land.

BOY

      I could step out, be Richard again,
      into insect sound on the riverbank

SARAH

Mayflies, dragonflies lazy over the grass
over the rippling water

BOY

      its clear hedgerowed surface. Wave rise
      and fall under bridges, back into shadows.
      The pasture's strange ride
      the current pulls us never yet
      the future, never quite.

SARAH

      tumbling over streams
in late summer the fish in clear water.

BOY

      Meadows rear up beside me.
      Splashes of light. Wasp summer
      riding the bitter water.

SARAH

Cress in flower, birds catching
the pale hands of cow parsley

BOY

       foaming in the hedgerows.

SARAH

Ears of rushes, wildflowers, each chalky lip.
We are in our places

BOY

                  rising
      and falling in the water meadows.

SARAH

the slow trailing of the water weeds.

BOY

          beside us the world passing
      from its moorings, a drifting ribbon
      either side along its way.

SARAH

The trees decked in flowers
above flinty gravel.

BOY

      Oh! Sarah the five pence it is all spent

SARAH

Five pence?

BOY

      I am in a boat rowing
      along cool green banks, the river of my home? Yes?

SARAH

Is all well Richard?

BOY

> That faithful step out where the waters rush
> to meet a body living on nothing but air.
>
> This soft, desolate green.
> Oh! is it water or land Sarah?
> Everything slides past rough-headed
> in these ragged waters.

SARAH
Richard, Richard what ails you?

BOY

> The raised armada, the steely flash.
> I see his eyeballs, for what is his rivalry
> upwards into His jut
> (for someone pours the weathers across us).
> His keeper and wayfarers, his waterspouts
> join my waterspouts, my eyelets do fill

SARAH
Calm yourself, tell me what is happening?

BOY

> Not early hair grass or sheep's sorrel.
> Not hedge mustard or mugwort
> Not rough grass reeds and codlins.
> Not marsh watercress or toadflax
> Not mulleins or soapwort,
> Not Ox-tongues, or heaven forbid
> the sweet stench of mignonette
> but bird-egging and blackberries
> apples and pears in windfalls
> and cob nuts in pocket-fulls.

IN MEADOWS AND RUINED GARDENS

Water mirrored with light
dark-haired and dark-eyed
through the watercress beds
Richard and Sarah.

Crows in white chalk fields
spider-silk and flowers
no path or milestones where
dragonflies jewel the stream.

Trout in the middle of the day
drink the river ripples
into diamonds over their gills
upstream in cool refreshment.

Weather moves through
the meadows over Richard
and Sarah, beside bugle and ladies
bedstraw, it swims over trout

at rest in the shade.
Their diminishing shadows
the migrant birds rise to the sky
never to return.

Afloat in the waterlilies
in meadows and ruined gardens
Richard and Sarah
breathe the weightless air.

Wind, lifts above the water.
Stained glass shines in the river
as the moon sings to the forest
of hop flowers and apple-boughs.

BOY

> I dreamt that we were dancing, you
> and me Sarah, in a strange mechanical way
> like the automaton we saw at the fair.
> And we danced among side-tables laden
> with platters of luscious fruits
> and of sliced meats
> and cut-glass jugs of crystal water.
> A small boy lost among the adults
> came to me. When I lifted him
> he was wet through and crying.

MATE

> He was not really fully in his body
> at this time. He was dying or dreaming.
> Or dreaming of dying. The sea
> water he had drunk (and we warned him
> not to) overtaking the sweetness
> of his waters. Bitter salt
> in the blood turning him feverish.

CAPTAIN

> If there is no vessel by the morrow
> the boy must be killed.

> *Richard is on the trout path, water lazy into the wind.*
> *Rippling and watery places sleepwalk the body*
> *a forest mirrored: water, birds, sky, flowers*
> *drink it, half in the world and half not. Beneath*
> *the faithful boat there is death and early windfalls.*
> *Water not wildflowers ragged. His summer step*
> *: the nothing of shadow. Sky beside clouds*
> *this upstream world: river, heaven.*
> *And the bugle that will meet the half jewel spread*
> *in tumbling waters beside bruised hedgerows.*
> *Richard rises, music sending him home*
> *over the meadows.*

CAPTAIN

My eyes scan forward to the bows
searching the horizon for ships.

Save us Oh Lord, or else we perish.

Richard your time has come.

BOY

No, No, not me sir
No.

Though he slay me, yet will I trust in him

MATE

A penknife
carves deep into living wood.
Slices an apple, removes the core
so only pure white flesh remains.

The master's arm a weapon.
I see the quick slash across his throat
and the knife glint in the sun.

The blade bites open a long red welt
our faces greedy, shining
the blood to startle and surge.

How it was over
an opening and a closing.
And how it was only just begun.

Three adults and a half.
The boy, slumped Asks 'why me?'
until the knife answers.

His wound a mouth to our mouths.
Fatal. We press open, kiss,
his feverish neck.

Our own bodies brace against
him in our embrace
carnal and corporeal.

Oh! How we eat and drink.
Witness our own bloody
mouths as we turn away.

Each a leering smile
to match his wound.
His blood a flood, a sacrament.

Drained, pale, the bones
and sinews. He is become
a carcass for butchering.

Only the sun and the wind
caress his body.
A gash opens another world.

SHIP-STORY

Come away lad, strange storms and fearful days
a slow hunger homes-sure the blood.
Captain, Captain! The storm wave by which you sank
four good lives are specks
'as she, tossed and rose the never'. Days wrecked
days since *Mignonette*, forgive me, foundered went.

The sailors sail alone the sailor's sea and sun.
Alas for Atlantic men when weather is so thirsty.
Crew must will limbs and fearful sharks surround.
Between his hunger, the poor ill-fated boy.
Starving, mad, alone, their will be done.
They kill! The boat smaller now an open grave.

Pierced. He lay, death an ocean terrible, for all.
God then but slowly tell the poor boy's story
this open lad, a poor slashed death. Captain
of the in between. What sufferings
laid the lad in such a ravenous way
the sailors oh! his limbs at last they bless.

NED

After that act
we are monstrous with power
and peril.

We are on terms
with the ferryman. Eye him
across the expanse of water.

And the thing unclean
no longer whole or animate
in the bottom of the boat.

We gag with horror
with dread and revulsion and relief
bruised flesh falling from the bone.

Water pushes through the boards.
This darkness we lean into
has dissolved the light.

Fish writhe under us as we struggle
with our souls, Flood takes the helm.
Oh! we have become as monsters.

In dismemberment and restoration
we are Richard embodied.
There's nothing to say

for I see my own mortal flesh
between the living and the dead
– the sacred and profane.

CAPTAIN

We thought it better to kill the Boy and drink the drops of blood [with the assistance of our shrouds]. I offered up a prayer for his soul [our rash act, it must be done, it may save three lives]. We then set to work. The poor Boy never moved nor spoke a word, in five seconds he was breathless, we caught the drops of blood and divided it the best we could. And it was a blessing to us.

Why the sun a fatal greed?
Why the muscles in sacrament?
One downward slash through skin
kissed bones, feverish over mouths
and opening, he carves a wound.
Blade raised so bodies open their surge and welt.
Kill to drink as blood drops
and lean him, wreckage against horror. The horizon
falters, dismembered. While they with red smiles
weapon our own misery, our mortal moved expanse
must into revulsion our act unending.
A body brutal night, cut they the hull of it
in late tenderness, feasting, on sorrowful flesh.

NED

From one frail vessel
to one frailer
we are alive again
though the way falters.
The horizon open, unending.
What other choice offers?
Between the living
and the dead
we are part of the wreckage
alive on the entrails of another.
My own mortal flesh
and the indifferent ocean beyond.

CAPTAIN
We cut off his Clothes and very soon afterwards we are feasting on
the fleshless body, washing the remainder and covering it up out of
the Sun until another day.

MATE
      The body warm and fevered
      his throat not merely cut but bruises appeared
      and upon his arms some deep indentations.

      We fell upon the blood with brutal ferocity
      but the sun hastened the tender decomposition
      so we must wash the meat in brine to cleanse it.

NED
      The same night he was betrayed
      he was a broken thing painful to look upon
      (was that someone leaving or just the wind
      getting up?). Baleful, though it was, it was us
      that did him harm. And there was nowhere
      for this remnant, apart from where he lay.
      No ceremony given, but for the repetition
      of the sun in the morning and of the stars
      at night. A sorrowful tenderness of waves
      beating against the hull of the body,
      which is broken for his blood.
      And broken, become a thing.
      A breath of air stirring overwhelms

      the body: fragile vessel of all our hope.

BEFORE IT IS TOO LATE

Anybody
Anything
Have you anything for me?

In the afternoon
How long ago?
Very bad weather.

Before dark
Before tomorrow
Before it is too late.

There is no chance
The distance is too great.

LETTER TO PHILIPPA DUDLEY WIFE OF CAPTAIN TOM DUDLEY FROM HIS AUNT MARY IN SYDNEY
26th July 1884

We have no news of Tom and now that he is on his way to us I still take note of snippets of news you may enjoy or will miss. Sadly, the British flag was hoisted in Stellaland but subsequently pulled down by the inhabitants. Also, that various Australian colonies are adopting addresses to the Queen praying for the Federal Council Bill. Here the business does well, and although we are busy, we are thriving and happy. No more letters, next time we speak it will be face-to-face as once Tom is here and settled, he will be able to call for you to come.

Part the Fourth

in which
the remaining sailors are rescued
returned and put on trial

24° SOUTH AND 27° WEST

CAPTAIN

Nights without a shower of rain passing over us.
The poor Boy's remains getting Strong in Flavour
disjointed his back leg, dipping it overboard and cutting
any bad. We had still some left when Ned Brooks steering
cryed:

NED

'a Sail'

CAPTAIN

Almost senseless
and unable to stand, we prayed the stranger
may cross our path.
We saw she was Bearing
and managed a little strength to row to windward
to be near them. In an hour and a half we saw
them bear down on us and offered thanks to God
and in very little time we were fast alongside.

We being helpless the crew got us on board.

*The German Barque, Moctezuma, cargo of nitrate from Punto Arenas,
bound for Hamburg.*

MATE

We were hauled aboard the Barque *Moctezuma*
on ropes like cargo

ERICH WIESE

just bags of bones.

CAPTAIN

> Gentleman we board Bearing our distress and hardships
> our almost passage. Will Lady Barque *Moctezuma* stand to
> all crew must to tell them officers our thanks
> ordering England and saw over and managed the clothing
> and remains.
> Row as we seamen did, without
> Steering and Memory had in being our very boat.
> Thankful ever, God Keep us, but How through any cutting?
> We for ever had, to friends in strangers,
> sufferers of our senseless bound mouths Cryed and prayed.

MATE

> And were given water

NED

> and bread

CAPTAIN

> and meat.

ERICH WIESE

> I am ordered to the rowing boat
> to throw overboard dreadful scraps of flesh
> and gnawed shards of bone.
>
> God forbid
> any of our brother seamen endure the hardships
> of that poor soul.

LETTER TO CAPTAIN TOM DUDLEY FROM HIS
AUNT MARY IN SYDNEY
3rd September 1884

Still no news of you Tom, I hope all is well. I said I would
not write but I send this to your old house in case you have
had to turn back. Silver iron and copper lodes have been
discovered in the Barrier Ranges at Broken Hill and small-pox
continues to spread in Victoria. General Gordon has routed
the Arab insurgents. But here a serious outrage committed
by Blacks in the Northern Territory; three Europeans were
speared. Thank God a reprisal operation was carried out by
Mounted Constable George Montagu and took in Argument
Flat and Marrakai Station along the Mary River. Inspector
Paul Foelsche also led a reprisal party. A third, civilian, party,
known as the 'Hauschildt Rescue' party, was armed by the
Government but not accompanied by any police.

I worry for you, write to me when you receive this.

toiling, head balancing
a slow swung chain
the knots up full clinking
linking iron collars

Sat 6th September 1884

On a day mostly cloudy, some squalls and showers, a south-westerly breeze blowing the Moctezuma arrives with the survivors at Falmouth Harbour.

> *And over the red beds of maerl and shipwreck*
> *squalls of Light Flashes an unfettered sou'wester*
> *the survivors today at Falmouth are home*
> *and Harbour safe*

Richard is not among them. He did not come home.

On board Falmouth pilot, Gustavus Lowry Collins, guides them through the wide estuary of the River Fal to dock at Falmouth Harbour.

CAPTAIN

A PRAYER TO SAINT ANTHONY
OF LOST THINGS

The peninsula stretches out its neck
out to open water. High cliffs and a sou'wester
behind us. We see the Black Rock
but the sea obeys the wind's command
and we clear the Manacles unfettered to enter
into anchorage of Falmouth Harbour, safe
under the eye of Saint Anthony of lost things
his regular revolving clockwork mechanism
and successive Flashes of Brilliant Light.

DEPOSITIONS TAKEN IN FALMOUTH on 6th SEPTEMBER 1884
at the Customs House on the Quay.

CAPTAIN

At the time of sailing the ship was tight and staunch, in every way fit for the voyage.

NED

The 16th day or night after the shipwreck the boy got ill. Lots were not agreed to, and I said 'Let us all die together.' I objected at all times to casting lots, I should not like to kill anyone and I should not like anyone to kill me.
On the 19th day Dudley said there would have to be something done.

MATE

I agreed with the Master it was absolutely necessary one should be sacrificed to save the rest. The Master selected Richard Parker, boy, as being the weakest.

NED

I heard a little noise and looked around and saw the boy was dead. I fainted away just after for a minute or two

I feel Us kill the boy until Dudley and blood.
Saw the lad was dead. Fainted
Let I   ...I flesh
a knife. Sore were flesh, I sucked a thirst
sitting congealed, subsisted and swollen.

One could cut all away and still we could have died.

...I looked around and saw Dudley catching the blood from him & I asked him for some, he gave me some quite congealed, I sucked it down as well as I could. Dudley was standing over the boy bending over him. Stephens was steering the boat, I saw the boy's neck was cut and I couldn't tell how, I did not look enough. I saw the knife soon after, there was blood on it.

CAPTAIN
And the rest subsisted on the flesh until the 24th day, the 29th July.

NED
I knew the Captain had killed him because he said so himself. Stephens told me he was steering the boat when the Captain killed the boy. I shared his blood and flesh with the others. We were all in a terribly bad state, very thin and weak. We were getting sore by sitting, our feet were very much swollen we did not feel the hunger so much as the thirst.

The lad was in a great deal worse condition than any of us, I think he was dying. But for the death of the boy, I believe we should have died of hunger and thirst.

DANIEL

In front of the magistrates in Falmouth on 8th September they were remanded until 11th September. I may be Richard's brother but I'm also a seaman. When I appeared in court on the 11th and shook hands with the three survivors of the Mignonette there was a gasp from the gallery. They were then further remanded until the 18th September.

John Burton, who owns the Old Curiosity Shop at the top of the High Street in Falmouth stands bail, £400 for Dudley, £400 for Stephens, and £200 for Brooks, for their trial in Falmouth. A thousand pounds in all. For this he is presented with a gold snuff box by the citizens of London.

THE OLD CURIOSITY SHOP

John Burton, at your service. Purveyor of curios
and curiosities from all across the globe.
Here, at the top of Falmouth high street
I have some scrimshaw work on whalebone
the usual unicorn horn displayed in a vitrine
sailing ships in bottles, shells and beadwork
and an orator's chair from Cannibal Islands.
I have Delft shoes, glazed hats and round
jackets, embroidered weskits & some salty
tales, string work, anchors and iron rings
jade ornaments, red and black lacquer work
a telescope, sundry tea pots and silk kimonos
spice boxes, novelty tobacco pipes, a mounted
elephant skull, a papier mâché carnival mask
an exquisite collection of South American moths.
The town is behind the men, the whole country
sympathises. This is the perfect moment to
make my name and bring in business. For I have
a handsome set of antlers, a complete set
of Chinese fingerguards, a lady's travelling case.
What else? Let me see: a gilded birdcage,
an ostrich egg, a stuffed Dodo, a diving helmet
a complete human skeleton (we ask no questions)
some hammered silver coins and a painted fan.
In short, my emporium attracts all the skiffskaff
objects the riffraff merchant sailors bring me.

*Captain Dudley spends the week out on bail 11th–18th September 1884,
at home with his wife and three children in Sutton, Surrey. Stephens
and Brooks, having no money to return home, are put up at the Sailors
Home in Falmouth near the Customs House and Docks until their fares
can be found. In lovely September weather, mostly dry and warm, Mate
Edwin Stephens is holed up at a tavern called the Chain Locker after
the unexpected turn of events as slosh, slush, goes the soft slop and slap of
slack tide…*

THE CHAIN LOCKER

The Customs House scares me
with its grand porticoed entrance, its thick rock walls
the confiscated brandy kegs under lock and key.

We've been told we will all be charged
We're like small boats tied up and sitting on their keels
on the mud of low tide. For now, at least I'm snug

in the Chain Locker a pint of bitter in my hands.
At dusk I watch the Custom's officers haul by rope
the lanterns to hang from each salt bitten lamp post.

Crayfish and crab baskets, crates of ropes
and piled nets. Trapped by a stifling closeness
the word is out and townsfolk are agog with the news.

JIMMY MORRISON RESIDENT OF FALMOUTH
They ate his heart first,
though that don't bear thinking about.
The other sailors (Tom Dudley is,
on account of his being teetotal, elsewhere)
and here's one
particularly fond of his drink.

*Falmouth – 19th September 1884. It's a dry day, some sunny intervals
but cloud and fog for a time in the afternoon. An easterly breeze blows
over the hillside town and across the docks. There is a hearing before the
magistrate in the Town Hall on the High Street. An hour before the start
a great crowd is assembled around the entrance. In a large oblong room
with tall arched windows filled with fresh sea-light, the noise of the streets
comes in…gossip and footfalls, and some street sellers working the crowd
and eager to sell their wares.*

Edwin Stephens and Ned Brooks arrived in Falmouth yesterday evening and Dudley by the morning mail train. Captain Thomas Dudley has recovered his robust and vigorous form, only the Mate Stephens remains marked by traces of recent sufferings.

Ned Brooks turns Queen's Evidence and testifies for the prosecution against the Captain and Mate with his own charges dropped. The prosecutor's request surprises all, including Ned Brooks.

NED

We had been told we will all be charged with murder.

At dusk the Custom's officers haul by rope
the lanterns, hanged from each salt bitten post.

SEARGEANT LAVERTY ON HIS OATH SAITH
>I arrested Captain Dudley under warrant.
>He seemed surprised and shewed Excitement
>He wanted to have the knife as a keepsake.

ROBERT CHEESEMAN COLLECTOR OF CUSTOMS
ON HIS OATH SAITH
>Dudley Said we've come to make our Statements.
>
>I ask each one 'Is that a true statement?'
>The prisoners separately Yes, 'yes.'
>About a lad, said did open him.
>Boat days, and saw not days
>but endless. Mentioned bone to him
>mentioned knife of an instant
>next the flesh was stripped.
>Each agree they wanted blood
>OATH them said in statements
>and the pieces there eat better
>said Captain offering the heart
>presenting me the rib.

SAMUEL JOHN LOUTTIT TRESIDDER CLERK
ON HIS OATH SAITH
>I did not caution either of them
>I had not the remotest idea
>a crime was alleged against them.

ERICH WIESE GERMAN SEAMAN
ON HIS OATH SAITH
>A boat one morning at 10am and we was toward it
>I could not said what sort of flesh or bone it was
>we were too excited to ascertain.
>I surprised from the Captain, two paddles, crutches
>chronometer, a sextant and some clothes.

RICHARD HODGE LICENSED WATERMAN
ON HIS OATH SAITH
> From the Captain of the *Moctezuma*
> the items as said and a list in German
> I handed all to Sergeant Laverty.

GUSTAVUS LOWRY COLLINS TRINITY PILOT
ON HIS OATH SAITH
> After the Captain mentioned me into the Cabin
> in the boat he told four. I asked him what used
> the other one.
>> He said (the boy cast nearly dead)
> 'Would it not better that we should do the Boy?
> So, the Captain appear to the boy, who be lying
> at the bottom of the boat, his arm over his face
> (he is me, the position of the arm). Yes, my boy,
> I helped my knife in there, cut it came and had out
> his liver and heart. The blood we drink of the bailer.'

Out on the streets there are murder ballads and public sympathy.

NOW ON VIEW
THE BOAT
OF THE MIGNONETTE
in which the crew of the yacht lived for 24 days after the
foundering of the vessel.

On exhibition at the London & South-Western Hotel, Paul Street.
The proceeds will be devoted to meeting the expenses of Captain
Dudley and Mate Stephens at the forthcoming trial at the Assizes.

ADMISSION SIXPENCE

JIMMY MORRISON
They say you can even see the bloodstains.

LETTER TO CAPTAIN TOM DUDLEY
FROM HIS AUNT IN SYDNEY

8th September 1884 – Oh Tom I have intelligence of a disaster to the yacht *Mignonette*, owned by Mr. J. Want of Sydney, the survivors enduring great privation and resorting to cannibalism. I am revolted by the disclosures but thank God that you are alive. In your weakened state I pray that given time you will be thoroughly recruited back to health. I urge you to remember your prayers, for the Lord God, knowing everything saw your suffering and will forgive you. Though I know not what to say to the neighbours.

On a dry and sunny day after a frosty start, on 3rd November 1884 the trial opens before a Judge, Baron Huddleston, in the city of Exeter.

THE MARK OF CAIN

Did it amount to murder?
Here where Judge Jeffries conducted his Bloody Assizes
the scaffold there outside the court.
Captain Dudley rushes from the morning's mail train.
No more than a glimpse of the cathedral down Broadgate
exhibitors at the Apple Fair packing up in Lower Market.
On the list: Sarah Ley for feloniously slaying Francis Ley;
Joseph Jasper Richards alias Joseph Richard Jasper
for bigamy; John Bray for burglariously breaking
into a dwelling house; and a slaying at sea.

The cells newly furbished but narrow, confining and low.
They are brought in around the raised bench to the hall
before the Honourable Sir
Knight, Baron of the Exchequer,
and Justice of the High Court.
                              The newspapers saying:

The ghastly means by which they preserved their own lives
so they will forever bear upon their brow the mark of Cain.

            An outrage upon human feelings…
            Nothing more horrible and revolting…
            Our shuddering abhorrence…

PHILIPPA DUDLEY
            Think on the dreadful tortured positions of the castaways.
            What evidence against the prisoners
            apart from their own confessions?

            Lord lay not this sin to their charge.

EXETER QUARTER SESSIONS – WINTER ASSIZES

Be it remembered on the first day of November in the year
of our Lord one thousand eight hundred and eighty-four
Thomas Dudley and Edwin Stephens came to the Winter Assizes
at the Castle of Exeter to the use of our Lady the Queen

    for the crime of murder of Richard Parker

    with force and arms on the High Seas
        within the Jurisdiction of the Admiralty
           wilfully and with malice aforethought

against the Peace of our said Lady, her Crown and Dignity.

If there is a conviction before Judges of her Majesty's High Court
then for surety one hundred pounds each in good and lawful money
and if they fail, levied of their goods, chattels, lands and tenements

be void or else stand in full force and virtue.

PROCEEDINGS

By means and methods
>   they shall better knowst the truth.

All Treasons and Trespasses, Contempts and Concealments
Rebellions, Riots, Routs and Retentions
Confederacies, Counterfeitings, Clippings and False Coinings
Maintenances, Misprisions, Manslaughters and Murders
Killings, Burglaries, and Rapes of Women
Unlawful Assemblies and Unlawful Uttering of words
and all other evil doings, Offences and Oppressions
Injuries and Insurrections.

Crown Exhibits A–E

Ships Registration: *Mignonette* 56845 built 1867
Agreement and Account of the Crew: Agreement No. 87274 dated
15th May 1884
Account of Changes in the Crew of Foreign-going ship before final
departure from the United Kingdom 16th May 1884.
?
Penknife

MR COLLINS FOR THE DEFENCE

Their lips were dry and black
their tongues were hard as stone

Horrible as the repast was
Disgusting as the food was

This act was a necessity
it saved their lives.

Richard Parker lay there dying
these men had wives and families.

And but for his sacrifice
they would all have died.

JUDGE BARON JOHN WALTER HUDDLESTON SUMS UP

With every feeling of sympathy
you hold yourself to a duty which is to be discharged.
It might be urged that this was self-defence
yet where was the danger at Parker's hands?
He was lying for some hours at the bottom of the boat.
The peril lay in the violent assault of hunger
and of thirst. It could not be self-defence.

I find no authority
in the recognised treatises on the criminal law
where murder is excusable on the ground of necessity.
I know of no such law as the law of England.

> To preserve one's life is a duty
> but duty often requires sacrifice
> of one's own life.

Your duty, Jury?
Whether the facts so found amount to murder.

THE JURY FOREMAN DELIVERS A SPECIAL VERDICT

More than of life, or chance, or the fourth day
or of the four, I thought instead of the knife
to my throat, if I were the one. Body and blood
if someone must feed the men.

He was just a boy!

But whether the prisoners are guilty of murder
the jury are ignorant and refer to the Court.

London – 4th December 1884

The trial is moved yet again, this time to the Old Bailey to be tried under the Lord Chief Justice. Control of the sea, that artery of Empire and of Trade its life-blood, is of paramount interest to the Government. On a mostly cloudy day with squalls and showers, not least in the legal argument amongst the assembled judges, a fresh SW breeze increases to near gale force and swirls around to the NW. The Lord Chief Justice's assistant in the robing rooms is licking his lips...

A LURID TALE

A lurid tale my Lord
and upon the tenderest flesh.
It is on everyone's lips.
Yet when he came to it
one of the sailors realised
he just couldn't stomach it.
But such a juicy story
of the captain and the mate
every newspaper relishing
sinking their teeth in the meat
of such a scandal.

The court is densely crowded, the prisoners are brought up, soon everyone will know and it will be a lesson to them.

The Lord Chief Justice places the black cap upon his head to read the sentence of death.

THE LORD CHIEF JUSTICE
      For each
      all regrets and possibilities dip
      his words an iron grating
      closing the eye of the mind
      darkening, the sun behind a cloud.

After the solemn words are said, in sympathy, the judge tells the prisoners they should plead for mercy.

THE LORD CHIEF JUSTICE
      Every man, woman and child
      in this world must view you
      with pity.

      Awful and miserable
      for famine, despair, cold and heat
      had done their worst.

So, they pled for mercy:

      CAPTAIN TOM DUDLEY in a low voice.
then
      MATE EDWIN STEPHENS in broken sentences.

LETTER TO CAPTAIN TOM DUDLEY
FROM HIS YOUNG RELATIVE IN SYDNEY

I send this letter to your wife to pass on to you in prison, but I do not know if you are receiving them. And now on 8th December I read both you and Stephens, captain and mate of the yacht *Mignonette*, are sentenced to death in England for murder of the boy Parker, who was killed and partly eaten (to think I am even writing these words!).

I pray to God the Queen will pardon you and enclose a recent family photograph we had made specially.

My mother says I must comfort you that the business in Sussex street is still available.

The Press Association is officially informed that the Secretary of State for the Home Department has advised the Queen to respite the capital offence passed on Thomas Dudley and Edwin Stephens. They must now wait until the further signification of Her Majesty's pleasure.

And what of the Honourable Jack Want, Sydney Barrister and Politician, owner of the Mignonette? Where is he while Thomas Dudley and Edwin Stephens languish in goal and Ned Brooks tries to rebuild a life? He makes a scrapbook for his newspaper cuttings of the trial, but in the Antipodes it's the summer season of yachting on Sydney Harbour and there is plenty to enjoy being out on the water.

A QUIET ANCHORAGE

Becalmed, we start to fish. Silver and bastard
trumpeter, mackerel, rock cod, and sharks. On the
sandspit flathead, on the kelp perch.

A Lighthouse on a small island with swarms of geese.
Double the size of a grey goose and the flesh on the breast
...resembled more nearly a sirloin of beef.

Four fathoms beautifully clear. An hour of daylight left
we put down our nets and at once have half a boatload
of beautiful crayfish.

A white sandy beach for morning and evening swims.
Days of shooting: ducks in the lagoons, kangaroos, rabbits
and penguins in their burrows.

At the sound of the foghorn we return to dine and smoke
until the sport grows monotonous.

Jack wants what Jack wants.

London – 13ᵗʰ December 1884
In the short gloomy days of Winter, London is now cool and mostly cloudy. The day starts with some drizzle and a gentle SW breeze and a letter from the Home Office that recommends to her Majesty to commute the sentence to six months imprisonment without hard labour.

On 15ᵗʰ December 1884 the newspapers report:
> Great disappointment is felt by the prisoners at Holloway and their friends at the decision.

Neither Dudley nor Stephens felt they had done anything unusual or wrong, it was the sailor's risk.

CAPTAIN

> But didn't I bring them
> back to land when the yacht
> was lost at sea?

PHILIPPA DUDLEY

> From the first
> he never dreamed he would be punished.
> All our savings are gone in his defence.
> No pardon, no immediate release.

> Yes, for me it is a painful surprise.

THE MIGNONETTE PRISONERS—Mrs. Philippa Dudley, wife of the captain of the yacht *Mignonette*, has by permission of the Home Secretary, had an interview with her husband in Holloway. Captain Dudley was, like ordinary prisoners, behind an iron grating and much agitated. He had nothing to complain of, he had occupation to relieve the monotony, and should carefully observe the regulations. On learning that a near relative of his in Australia, of whom he had not heard for many years, had written to him and enclosed a photograph he became very excited and wanted very much to see the likeness. In the course of the conversation Dudley alluded to his intention of settling in the colonies and engaging in a business which has been offered to him. He gave expression to a fear that he would lose it on account of his incarceration.

Part the Fifth

in which
the prisoners are released
and Captain Tom Dudley suffers
an unexpected fate

THE ITCHEN LAD

An Itchen lad, an orphan,
he brought him to his death
for they must drink and sup.

For they must drink and sup.
He used his penknife on his throat
and all he said 'What, me?'

And all he said 'What, me?'
Four hands and no boat in sight
What could they do but kill?

What could they do but kill?
And when the rescue came
there's nought but a rib to show

There's nought but a rib to show
It was tide turn for the cabin boy
just an Itchen lad, an orphan.

London – 20th May 1885 Captain Dudley and Mate Edwin Stephens are released unexpectedly early to avoid public interest, into the morning of a cloudy day, cool with light shower and a gentle Southerly breeze.

PHILIPPA DUDLEY
I organised a neighbour to care for the children while I was gone to London to meet my husband. But he was released an hour before the time so I miss him and must return home.

CLEMENCY

A year and a day from the day they sailed
the yacht's wake had swallowed lives.
As if prison pulled them below the waterline
and they sunk behind scuttles and deadlights.
Their lost year, asleep on a bed of water.

Set free from a beginning that became an end
they are released as from an enchantment.
A Liberty man with a ticket of leave, Captain Dudley
looks into sunlight, feels in clemency a Southerly.
A free man now, with Sydney in his sights.

Captain Thomas Dudley, his wife Philippa Mary and their three young children, Winifred, Julian and Elizabeth, arrive from London to Sydney on the 1 October 1885 onboard the Austral. They soon established themselves with a ship's chandlery business in the city, and a yacht building business at their home in Drummoyne, on the harbour foreshore at the point with Five Dock Bay. Notices of their businesses are published in the local Sands Directory of Sydney

Dudley T. R & Co., oilskin, sail, tent
tarpaulin and flag-makers, yacht &
boat outfitters and riggers, 47–51
Sussex st.

Dudley Thomas, Captain, yachtbuilder,
Cambridge rd, Drummoyne

To his customers and neighbours, he remains Cannibal Tom. He is notorious, known but never known. His fresh start, his survivor's story. In compression and exhalation, the sunshine turns the streets to air and water, to the various blues that are never enough. Here, on the harbour, Sydney Harbour, Tom Dudley is a family man, at home in flat acres of briny light that shines on Cambridge Street and Sussex Street, both named for the old country (as if he had never left).

ANTHONY HORDERN'S FOR BUCKLES & BRACES
'BROIDERIES & LACES

ANTHONY HORDERN'S FOR STONES & HONES
& MILLS FOR GRINDING BONES

MARY DUDLEY
Well I never!

THE TENDEREST FLESH

Alone in the hot night air Tom Dudley
stands in scented curls of wood shavings
under the ribs of the new-built *Volunteer.*
What could have been? That old country
turning away under dark clouds.
But how many mansions in my Father's house
the streets running with rain, the figs
noisy with bats.

The children
are in their beds asleep
candle light flickers at their windows.
His flesh and bone
their young skin pale as milk.

In the shadows Philippa Dudley watches the man who returned home.

CANNIBAL TOM IN SYDNEY

For his charges and pains in the tragedy
Cannibal Tom, his feet on dry land
works as a chandler, has shelves of halyards
and hoists, rowlocks and rudders. Plain sails
through stanchions and swivels, rigging pins
and mast fittings. The wind still at his back
the harbour at his window.

Sailors come in for their transom pintles
and gudgeons, for blocks and jammers,
and lacing eyes, seacocks and furling gear.
His inventory of tangs and tins of tar
of cordage and netting. He sells them
                blue skies and fair weather
                trade winds and calm seas.

From the safe harbour of his chandlery
among splicing tools and shackles, here
his winch handles to lift you from the ocean
the necessary storm covers and the shrouds.
Don't press him about the shipwreck
or the endless days adrift, but ask gently
he will demonstrate the correct use of bailers.

Mate Edwin Stephens sails to keep himself from home. Able Seaman Ned Brooks 'no longer able' he will not go on the water. Both their families in a state of beggary and want.

NED

I do see him. Boy Parker. At night. The wife and the neighbours complain I cry out.

His drained eye. He is there split from his throat to his belly. All his organs outside his body glistening, ugly and alien. And he is gesturing to me, for he cannot speak, and I realise he wants me to put them back. And I think what are they? And where do you put them? And in which order do you slip them in back through that terrible wound?

And what of those consumed? Where do they lie?

PHILIPPA DUDLEY (reading from the newspapers)
The Intercolonial Yacht Race at Port Phillip, the Prize a cup valued at
£400 plus a golden anchor valued at £100, 23rd November 1888.
Sydney entries were J. H. Want's *Miranda,* a forty-ton centre-board
yawl, built in 1888 by W. Langford at Neutral Bay to a design by
Walter Reeks. She was unable to compete due to damage sustained
on the voyage down.

But the outstanding yacht of that year was *Volunteer,* a 33 ton, deep
keel yawl, captained by T.R. Dudley and built by him at Drummoyne
for W.P. Smairl.

JACK WANT
> Some would-be critics
> without knowing anything of my
> *Miranda* have given their opinions
> (generally of an unfavourable character).
>
> How fast she is in comparison to other 40-tonners
> I do not know.
> She is as fast a boat as I have ever been in
> and as a sea-boat, I don't believe
> there is her equal in the world.

*Jack Want has turned to different adventures writing a serialised column
in the newspaper and gluing it into his scrapbook. He spends the hot
months of December, January, and February, holidaying on comfortable
steamers.*

CAPTAIN

> I cannot forget the bailing or the thirst
> they are still with me.
> But I am a practical man and not prone
> to fits of melancholy.

PHILIPPA DUDLEY (reading from the Government Gazette)

> Thomas Riley Dudley's Improved Canvas Water Filter
> and Cooler, is granted a New South Wales Patent
> number 4086 on 4th November 1892.

What of Edwin Stephens the Mate?

    Did a bit of sailing out of Southampton
    but he went downhill with the drink.

    Worn through and shaking, dreading
    the rent collector, the bailiffs at the door.

    Evening after evening he sits at the table
    not leaving the house, his head in his hands.

And Ned Brooks?
Joined a Fair as 'The Man who Ate Human Flesh' or 'The Cannibal of
the High Seas'. He lives, a sea-creature trapped behind glass waiting to
be lifted out into the coruscating air.

Was that singing? The pianola roll playing to itself?

> *Ned Brooks is lost in the body of something*
> *that swallowed him long years ago.*
> *He's working the charter and the goose fairs,*
> *the horse fairs and the mops. Competing for attention*
> *with Madame Electra, between the waxworks*
> *and steam driven carnival rides. He's in the freak show*
> *beside the menageries and circuses.*
> *Travelling to Wakes, lost in the crowds*
> *of pleasure-seekers on roundabouts and gallopers*
> *who gawp at contortionists and are love-struck by mermaids.*
> *The illusionists and tricksters.*
> *He watches people trade their dull lives in factories*
> *for sensation on Switchbacks and terror*
> *on the Ghost Train.*

NED

> At night after the revellers leave
> I walk the unbearable field pleading for refuge.
> I am not in control of this dream, it is in control
> of me. The open ground around me is a calm dark sea
> as I step over pegged ropes and the canvas flaps.
> He is here, waiting
> propped in the boat between water and sky.
>
> I would run away if I could, but he always follows
> (the futility of a locked door against this intruder)
>
> The wife has left but the neighbours still complain
> I cry out.

134

We are all still shipwrecked.
No rescue. It goes on and on
There is no closing his flesh.
His eyes are inside my body
trying to break me open.

19ᵗʰ January 1900

In a stifling Sydney Summer
the sun beats down.

The Quarantine vessels arrive.
Coaling stops, unloading stops.

Vessels hurriedly leave
with half their crew onshore.

The rats desert the ships,
then the fleas desert the rats.

Arthur, the Dudley's carter
the first to contract the disease.

PHILIPPA DUDLEY
…then I see them coming and, before you know it, they are pulling
out all the rubbish
          …and some of it not rubbish
                              …and burning everything they can.

The slums and shanties of the Rocks are to be dealt with.

PHILIPPA DUDLEY
          And we all know what that means! Demolished.

Of course, Tom is not at his best. He is fevered and pustules are
breaking out in his armpits and groin. There are big fires between
Margaret and Erskine Street and an order to close the Bonded Stores.
They say it's bubonic plague.

The population suffers
: panic and dread,
carbolic and sulphuric.
Sydney, under siege, a hell
of smoke and noise.

In three days
of nausea and dizziness
aching and delirium
Captain Tom Dudley
chandler and sailmaker
is the first of the dead.

His corpse is attended
with every precaution
to prevent infection.
The space in the coffin
filled with strong disinfectant
then wrapped fittingly
in a jacket of sailcloth.

For his final voyage
the coffin is removed
by water to North Head,
towed in a skiff
behind a launch
out into the darkness.
To be buried deep
in quicklime
in the quarantine ground.

WOOD & COMPANY, UNDERTAKERS & EMBALMERS,
WESTERN RD & EVANS ST, ROSELLE. TEL 5 BAL.

Funeral Director
for the burial at North Head Quarantine Station, Sydney of
Captain Thomas Riley Dudley.

High above the harbour, North Head,
entrance and exit
small-pox or plague ridden
the bodies are buried.

Here they record
> *[Names of the vessels]*
> *[Names of the dead]*

FROM A NEWSPAPER
> Mrs Dudley telegraphs from the quarantine station
> to the effect that she, assisted by her daughter,
> nursed her late husband in his recent illness, and
> Miss Maggie Beattie did not do so.

INCANTATION

In the ruin of my body
a shroud of sickness covers me.

The wind whistles my hinges
bolts can't hold out the hungry man.

       Do not enter my body.
       Do not break through.

Entered and eaten, traveller
of flesh and bones and sinews.

The hungry man asks
What have you given me to devour?

Flesh and bones and sinews. What is left?
A few foul scraps.

On the crushed surface of the sea.
The ferryman asks: Have you paid my fee?

Water shushes at the beach.
Hush, the waves say, now it is over.

And what of Ned Brooks?

Riven with guilt and insanity
his days and nights on the ocean

unchanging, sleeping the sleep
of the dead.

Down, down
into the swirling depths

again and again
he is cast up

onto the surface of the waters

last survivor.

POSTSCRIPT

It is the month of May again, the month Richard left…

Sarah Parker, my great-grandmother, the bobbins and pins of her lace-making strewn about her, lies on her bed in her triple-fronted house on Cambridge Road. It's just off The Avenue on Southampton Common where the Holiday Fairs are held. Her mind can travel even if her body cannot (she's been bedridden since a bout of pneumonia at the age of forty). The scent of roses comes in from the swags of rambling roses around her upstairs window. She's been married to Charles Eli these many years, a gardener with his feet on dry land, not a sailor of the sea. Her cousin Richard, in her memory, is forever young. She lies back relinquishing the lace and in her mind's eye she is standing on Pear Tree Green again, just above the village of Itchen Ferry. She has her back to the school and is looking at the Churchyard of the Jesus Chapel where Richard's memorial stone lies…

SARAH
    The wind rises and the waves respond
    surging forward and pulling back

SACRED
TO THE MEMORY OF
RICHARD PARKER
AGED 17
WHO DIED AT SEA
JULY 25th 1884 AFTER
NINETEEN DAYS DREADFUL
SUFFERING IN AN OPEN
BOAT IN THE TROPICS
HAVING BEEN WRECKED
IN THE YACHT MIGNONETTE

Though he slay me yet will
I trust in him. JOB XIII.15

Lord lay not this sin to
their charge. ACTS VII.60

ACKNOWLEDGEMENTS AND THANKS

to *The Australia Council* for a project grant that made travel, to the UK and to Sydney for the fundamental research, possible.

to the *KSP Foundation* for their *Published Author Residency* giving me uninterrupted thinking space at a crucial point in the development of the first draft of this manuscript.

Thanks to Professor Rosemary Hunter, University of Kent Law Department for sending me the report of the Appeal decision and pointing me to DPP 4/17 at the *National Archives,* Kew.

to John Davies at the *Exeter Guildhall* for taking me behind the scenes, not open to the public, to show me the prisoner's cells and Judge's Room behind the main hall.

to the staff at the *Hampshire Archives Centre* in Winchester for audio recordings of local sea shanties and contract documents relating to the Shipwright's Yard at Itchen Ferry.

to Rachel Ponting for her help at the *Devon Heritage Centre.*

to Pascal O'Loughlin at *The National Poetry Library,* London for suggesting useful poetry anthologies within the collection and arranging a visit to the broadsheet collection at the *English Folk Dance & Song Library.*

to Lauren von Bechmann at *The Museum of Childhood,* V&A Bethnal Green for allowing me to open a Victorian Era teaching box and look through all its treasures. Thanks to Elizabeth James at the *V&A* for putting us in touch.

to the staff at The News Room at *The British Library* for help with finding relevant newspaper articles.

to Ann Pond and the staff at the *Bartlett Research Library, National Maritime Museum,* Falmouth for their help on nautical references, transcripts of interviews with local residents who remember the Falmouth trial, and to the Museum itself for helpful displays including a boat being built in-situ.

to Penny Rudkin and to Vicki Green at the *Maritime and Social Studies Research Centre,* Southampton City Library for help on period maps of the Southampton Docks and Itchen foreshore.

to Mark Beswick at the *Met Office National Meteorological Archive,* Exeter, for historically accurate weather observations for 1884/5.

to Victoria Wilson at the *English Folk Dance & Song Library* for her help with broadsides, the mysteries of the ROUD system, and the phrase 'the tenderest flesh'.

to the *National Archives* in Kew for access to original documents in the Home Office file which meant I held in my hands the contract signed by Richard's mark, the drawing of the *Mignonette* by Thomas Dudley, and all of the original depositions given in Falmouth by the survivors.

to the staff of the *Old Quarantine Station*, North Head, Sydney: thanks.

at the *Australian National Maritime Museum* in Sydney thanks to Sally Fletcher for access to the Plague Diary and photographs of yacht parties on Sydney Harbour; and to Linda Moffatt and Karen Pymble in the Library for unearthing information related to Tom Dudley's shipbuilding and racing yacht captaincy that placed him as a rival to Jack Want in the Sydney yachting world.

to the staff in the special Collections area of *The Mitchell Library*, Sydney for their help in providing access to Jack Want's Scrapbook and the 1884 Rulebook of The Royal Sydney Yacht Squadron.

to the National Library of Australia for the wonder of their online digitised TROVE archive particularly for articles about shark attacks, the Chronicle of the Year 1884 from the *Argus* 3/1/1885, Bubonic Plague in Sydney and The Centenary Intercolonial Yacht Regatta.

The poem 'Cannibal Tom in Sydney' was longlisted for the Live Canon International Poetry Prize and published in their 2019 Anthology.

An early version of the manuscript *The Sorry Tale of the Mignonette* was shortlisted for the Dorothy Hewett Award 2019.

thanks to Cherry Smyth, G.C. Waldrep, Laurie Duggan, Rose Hunter and Kerry Kilner for their critical engagement with the text as it developed.

thanks to Jennifer Russell and Godfrey Offord for their suggestions and live lock-down read-through on Zoom

thanks to Philip Gross and John Goodby for reading the finished manuscript and for their comments,

and thanks to all the many others who helped me along the way.

to Cherry, Peppe and Luciano with love and thanks for a London home away from home.

to my family for being so interesting!

and to Kerry for being a steadfast anchor in the dark days of writing that followed my father's death.

REFERENCES

p.15   Sarah describes contents of Teaching Box V&A Museum of Child-hood.

p.18   Jack Want 'I'll seize their hats' – A true incident from the life of pirate Benjamin Hornigold 1680–1719. By contrast, Jack Want merely dressed as a pirate when sailing on Sydney Harbour.

p.20   the epigraph – Captain F.W. Hickson, Superintendent of Pilots, Lights and Harbours, Sydney 1863.

p.25   Quote italics – Royal Commission on Unseaworthy ships, Final Report, Vol 1, 1874.

p.27   Scale of Provisions – from the contract, National Records Office, Kew.

p.28   variant of *We're Homeward Bound.*

p.29   These 4 lines Traditional, sourced from audio file Radio Solent, Hampshire Records Office.

p.37   Trinity House patent obtained January 1782 for Needles Light-house.

pp.41, 54, 63 and 93 – are derived from SENTENCES Numeral Flags used to communicate taken from Royal Sydney Yacht Squadron Rule Book 1883–4 copy belonging to F.B. Lark Pleiades (State Library NSW).

p.47   This poem, *Running Before the Storm*, is a cut-up from *True Reportary of Wracke and Redemption of Sir Thomas Gates*, by William Strachey, published by Samuel Purchas, 1625.

p.48   Cut-up from *Shipwreck Index of the British Isles* Vol 2, Richard & Bridget Larn, and from *2000 Miles in a Forty-tonner*, J.H. Want, *Evening News*, Sydney 14 April 1890.

p.49   Green Sea: A vessel is said to be 'shipping it green' when solid masses of water are coming on board in a heavy sea, sweeping away anything not properly secured. (*A Seaman's Pocket Book*, Osprey, 1943).

p.69   Uses information from Southampton Wildlife Link's *A Natural History of Peartree Green* (1992).

p.89   SHIP-STORY is a loose re-arrangement of the contemporary ballad 1884/5 'Fearful Sufferings at Sea, Lad Killed and Eaten'.

p.92   Mate – Inspired by *The Works of Edgar Allan Poe*, Volume 1 (of 5) of the Raven Edition.

p.92   Ned – Adapted from Luke 22:19 and Mathew 26:26 (KJV).

p.99   His report documents 20–30 Aboriginal deaths, other contemporary reports suggest between 70–150 deaths. (See *Colonial Frontier Massacres in Central and Eastern Australia 1788–1930*, University of Newcastle).

p.99 The four lines below inspired by *Heart of Darkness*, Joseph Conrad, (1899).

p.103 Some of the objects described come from *The Old Curiosity Shop*, Charles Dickens.

p.108 Advertisment from *The Exeter and Plymouth Gazette*, Friday October 31, 1884.

p.110 from *The Exeter and Plymouth Gazette*, Friday November 7, 1884,

p.118 From Trewman's *Exeter Flying Post*, December 17, 1884.

p.118 *The Daily Telegraph*, London, Wednesday, December 24, 1884, Issue 9229, p.2.

p.129 'For his charges and pains in the tragedy': quote from Philippa Dudley in *A History of Southampton*, Rev. J. Silvester Davies, First Ed. 1883, facsimile edition 1989.

p.131 Jack Want – *Sydney Sails: the story of the Royal Sydney Yacht Squadron's First 100 years (1862–1962)*, P.R. Stephensen, Angus & Robertson, Sydney, 1962.

p.131 From '2000 Miles in a Forty-tonner' J.H. Want, *Evening News*, Sydney, 14 April 1890.

p.134 Information on 'The Man who ate human flesh' found in a transcript of an interview with Falmouth resident Jimmy Morrison held by the Bartlett Library, National Maritime Museum, Falmouth.

p.136 *The Sydney Morning Herald*, 1 Mar 1900, and a Plague Diary viewed at the Australian National Maritime Museum, Sydney.

p.138 Philippa Dudley – *The Sydney Morning Herald*, 26 February 1900.

p.139 This poem bears a debt to Assyrian Incantations from R. Campbell Thompson, *The Devils and Evil Spirits of Babylonia: Being Babylonian and Assyrian Incantations Against the Demons, Ghouls, Vampires, Hobgoblins, Ghosts, and Kindred Evil Spirits, Which Attack Mankind*, Vol. 1: *Evil Spirits*. London: Luzac, 1903.

p.141 The Postscript contains reminiscences of my mother speaking of her grandmother, Sarah Parker.

p.142 Inscription: churchyard of St Mary on Peartree Green.

Lightning Source UK Ltd.
Milton Keynes UK
UKHW010629120321
380218UK00001B/43